I0236201

The
Expectation of Seeds

By Minister C. D. Johnson

AN EXERCISE IN FAITH

SPIRITUAL POEMS FOR GODS' GLORY

Introduction

Expectation of Seeds

By C D Johnson

I must first give thanks to my lord and savior Jesus Christ, for His patience and His love for the world. I am also thankful for you, for taking this moment to review these humble pages. This work documents with the uses of poems, the heart and lessons of one man, but I know that many of us are linked by a single source. These pieces are intended to make you comfortable with growth and recognition, the growth and recognition of yourself and the tasks before you. Only GOD will ever truly understand our progress, so our primary concern is clear.

Becoming older can mislead us to believe that we are no longer in need of council, but some warnings just as some mistakes, are destined to be repeated. The crux of this earth world is to allow every soul an opportunity to uncover their heart. These poems are a collection of well intentioned short reminders. The first is that this clay existence is not your punishment or your reward. Please take a moment to consider the importance of gaining strength as we advance. I pray there is a reminder included that can be of aid for you. These are the kind of reminders that a family minister might provide. Often times, a small seed can grow with an unimagined strength and resolve, just a nudge can be like being shaken awake.

It is my prayer that these pages in some way aid in your quest. Be on notice that some direction will make itself yours, even if you don't decide by your will. It was written that all are not meant to see. While there is an option, don't default of your love just to shield your ignorance. It does not matter why you've delayed, God remains on His throne. These words may be the start on your scheduled elevation, please digest and grow.

Acknowledgements

The Expectations of Seeds

I wish to acknowledge the love and blessings of GOD our Father. There is thanks to many but the long suffering heart of our savior, is the creation of love and my reason to be better. I take this opportunity to thank the friends and family who have provided their shoulders for the support of this one so in need of help. My children, Delan Angell, Lacia Kanessa, and Clinton II, declared my back covered in the way that only someone who has your back can do. To my loving grandchildren Solomon Delancy and Ava Johnson, keeping me stronger. Thank you for the contributions of my siblings, Debra Kelly and Angell Jacobs, with all love to my god-children Kadari and Yasir Naj-Allah

I must call out for the acknowledgement of my sons of the heart Ryan Walters and Moe Sheldon. They have been instrumental in my practical understanding of the holy word and the righting of this vessel. Along with the love of my children, who form my reason to smile, I'm now able to taste the feast of my blessing. Exciting me daily, is the gift of living truly thankful. The driving force for this project is my service to GOD. I live installed for the protective instruction of all Gods' children. I pray for their blessings in the light as they cultivate from the seeds sown.

C. D. Johnson, Sr.

About the Author

Minister C D Johnson

Our particular experiences are never as dissimilar as we would like to believe. The intensity and fervor for our individual "row to hoe" feels to us as unique, mostly because we find difficulty sharing where had to be corrected or we've missed our mark. Loved one, this world finds us all pulling our lives from the same relative confusions. The progression of our spirituality has to be our own, comparing one to another would mean that someone must be lose, when the lost of His children is the lost God has not allowed.

I was born in Washington, DC, between the World War II and the Korean wars during a time when black ladies and gentlemen were only allowed to live their realities within our community, otherwise known as someone less. I matured as an angry black man, which is should be expected seeing the people I love disrespected as underlings when we are much more. My mother and father feared that my voice may cause me to be silenced, but leaving as an early victim was not my fate but it began my journey. I an energized by the thoughtful responses from the youth of this current generation, God please bless their continuing growth and strength of value. Young seedlings know the vigor to act when a fight has the sanction by being right.

Training to lead a Christian household necessitates our recognition of rational choice of our battles but there are few battles based on logic. This is a problem for most of us still, but missions should have completion. My mission, as a Minister of the One God, is as any warrior with a cause they are willing to die for. We enjoy our lives, with enthusiasm while we are young and the anxiety of our conclusion thereafter. These words are the lessons of my nearly seventy years, I pray that they germinate strongly with your understanding.

Table of Contents

The Expectations of Seeds

Antiseptic Act of Forgiving

By C D Johnson

At five, kindergarten was the class for our acknowledge of new

Our fresh indoctrination about what makes our space owned

Thus begins our revocable acceptance about what is our own

Introducing the concept that this world does not turn by our will or joy

This is where we first learn that shoes may be stepped on

 and not all words are of encouragement

A test of your composition, but we should not fear the trial

Within this experience, wounded feelings can render us vulnerable

Without some feelings means we've chosen to be dead

As our growth, the final product taste best

Criticality is unfortunate timing, later moments matter exponentially

For our own forgiveness, we must provide that which we require

Ignorance tries to make comfortable, unearned pardon of ourselves

While we harbor poisonous hostility for the world

Recognize, that which has been done by your will defines your work

The painful lessons of learning to forgive, elevates our purpose

We need this vantage point to understand where we should go

Careful what you call me

By C D Johnson

Social salutations are endearing, we unearth trust for those we've known

Endearing bonds grow comfortably more familiar with time

Finding strength via these connections, fortifying our forces has illusions

Sharing the work of this station, One has proven worthy of greater regard

Our misuses of these titles, may gleam a loss of respect

With no disrespectful intent, particular labels requite singular reference

The Reverend One was a defining path, fitting only where Christ has gone

Enduring clay experience followers knew Him simply as Rabbi

No title is ever exalted enough, even when spoken from our knees

Clay ministries are revered for good service, representing our connection

But ministers exist to symbolize our source, tutors of Gods' lessons

This fit for appropriate labels, each ministry must answer for its own

The disciples of my savior, were punished with deaths of the hated

Each taken still committed to Gods' resolution of faith

The title of disciple was not only special in its solitary meaning

These souls are special with understanding of their work

To walk the path of the Master, commits by strength of faith

Some labels carry monitory conviction

I feel need to pray at the warming thought of God

More than the prices paid, the unbridled love we cannot answer

Clay hold their clergy to a higher scrutiny than their mirror

But judgment is above our calling and a signal of our failing

If the torturous murder of GOD With Us refuses your respect

You are of the third and woefully mislead

When we employ a holy name of the One GOD, He suffers our cry

His dedication to listen requires we only call with substance

We are heard, so speak correctly when calling on my Father

The respect we show is only fed by that we feel

Be guided by the light you see, self elevation forms no service

Cherished

By C D Johnson

Of all this life's' incentives, no hunger exceeds parent with child

We defend with savage effort

Protecting our essences as though we're fighting for air

Every task is our obsession, care givers comfort is service

Those who are yet to know this blessing, won't see this from where they stand

Agonizing over minutiae, sets the range of a parents concerns

Wearing returned formula with the pride of a badge

This must surely be a madman, or a parent with child

When our response to failures of faith, is our failure to respond

How could our Father love such children as these?

With all the patients and tenderness these hearts can be fed

We are cherished in the flavor of love we reserved for our future

We ask to be forgiven our weakness, but our feebleness has not waned

The trail of our travels, documents the circles of this confession

We must first be care givers, as we receive the freshening of our hearts

Our Father will never fail us, but how will you respond in kind?

Young souls, must learn from first nipple

When we ignore our origin, we may omit that you cherish

Choice of Alters

By C. D. Johnson

Acclimated by logistics, we barter what we have, for that we want

Sometimes cost, exceeds our exchange

The path selected at this fork, will targets your destination

The outcome of these exchanges, is the way that you keep score

The perception of success floats us, but reality demands accounting

The accounting of your life credit is finite

Nothing regulated for your ease but often for your salvation

Not all the needs of the clay are written on their faces

There are quiet secrets of longing, for which they've set no price

Some scenarios work as trappings for the unaware

The second time in, earns you the label of fool

Addiction to anything beyond your reach

, ends with needing what you cannot have, GOD is at your call

Before you kneel, be sure you're kneeling before GOD

If you worship your partner so you won't be alone

, your happiness is not a device of the clay

If you pray to the needle that just may take your life

, the escape that you seek is in your Fathers' house

For your prayers to be answered, be sure to whom they're addressed

Clay Cycle Realities

By C D Johnson

From our commencement without warning, with screams your sole response

The questions of your condition need to be asked, but how?

The most blessed are nurtured in the marinade of family esteem

We arrive defined as a gift, a positive symbol of good love

During these days we seek enlightening clues to our meaning

We embrace our inverting silence, communication advances exposure

Caution can be a grand attribute, but some riddles require an answer

We pray we will be more, as we grow

After the entree of our experience, confidently we gain our small voice

It is not because of the bounty of our harvest, we're just stronger than before

During these days we seek enlightening clues for our meaning

Yet the answer today, is still not noticeably clear

We declare the resolve to stand for our position, but for what do we stand?

The facility to be of conscience, still requites your hand

We know we have more to give, should giving be our way

The uses we make of our valued teachings, denotes what we have learned

At this time you are fully grown and listening may not be your way

If your portion does not meet your fill, question the value of your diet

After enrichments, and your years are grouped by scores

Urgency vents anxiety you have need to shed

You found your time expended, for most your days alone

Life again confines you to an egg, where solitary concerns are your own

Those with love for you, will lack the valor to watch your ugly decent

This is not an absence of devotion, more that some truth hurts

The strength of the gray is greatest as we protect

So pretend not to notice expressions, as they oblige a smile for your comfort

Families nervously watch the time, marking evidence of your place

You show your passion, when you pretend not to notice

The discomfort has grown high enough for enjoyment, too far to enjoy

The real decline of our pillars, removes the foundation from our selves

It stays difficult to remain grown, when your structure is no more

Draw from past exposures for protection, tomorrows day will come

Our following times may not be ours, reality can be a fist

Dance with me for this time we are blessed, realistically, that's want we have

Disjointed Intellect

By C D Johnson

Clay people, relate best with highlights of their mirror

When genuine growth is dormant, pretending forms our crutch

Likely performances for the survival of our confidence

, but its' so demeaning to the truth

Every consideration is made relative to those of curbed sight

Even when we wish to know best, this is not always our truth

Guarded minds have filters, permitting selected inputs

Demanding delimited results

With our compounded causality from internal battle

communication requires more than meer words

We learn that serving as our own foundation is clearly meant for One

Without the rest provided for us, we have no place to stand

Contacting your source, clears clay distractions from your sight

Attempting life without the vision of our travel

documents the cause of our confusion

Façade of the Frightened

By C D Johnson

The stock response of the frightened, is to pretend that they are strong

Their fake display manufactures fake strength, where there is actually none

If sensitivities get slighted, you change from who you are

Living as the blow fish, puffing your person, to appear strong

In fact nothing's changed, whatever peril there was, there is

When we no long approach every event as our measurement, we are more

All will be the reward for the humble, but not from the force of their hand

Raising our tone never makes us right; it just foolishly makes us loud

Our focus should target where it is we're trying to go

But there's importance in how it is we arrive

The bravado of the hapless disappoints, demonstrating our fertility

Thankful, the power is in the hands of GOD, but fools can still cause harm

Our Father obliges only our gift of obedient love

In the giving of our selves we're strong in the protection of GOD

While responding as the blow fish, changes nothing at all

Family Balance

By C D Johnson

Our elevations most devious impediment,

  is our imposed constraint for our time in balance

Balance for our lives complicates, with the exponent of every layer

We will speak more honestly about this, when we understand how

Not all of our issues bleed black or white

Some hues are fashioned by their course

Your need of balance swells, with the complications of your yolk

The soreness of your head, documents your choice of path

Do you believe in the service that you give, is there still time for you?

When we digest focus, we pray for the wisdom of its placement

To focus on the limbs may mean our loss of the tree

There should be some special gift you wish to give

And more importantly, someone you wish for receipt

There are people who feel love for you, you don't consider

Here again another complication of the yolk

A person can only maintain the stability of two points,

  a family may have many more

To receive the touch you need, is only surpassed by providing it

Family

By C D Johnson

The circle of your protections has begun with yourself

Love of self delineates, the relativity of your embrace

While the swallow reach inward, each option feels personal

Surviving some encounters alone, simply means nobody lived

We make claim to multi-functions, our perceptions do miss lead

When your protection is for those in your arms, that's a godly start

This is the position where your family love is groomed

Our familiar tags, suggests we know these people

In most houses, surname is the functioning connection

Relationships that facilitate expectations, are often lacking in comfort

The gravitation of like spirits, should flow with ease

Feelings shared by joining ethics, shapes your factual kinship

If there is need to press, there is error in your connection

Reactions are not always good or not, but that's just who we are

Your totality is not solely of your blood, we're too complex for that

There are love ones of other names, you preserve as family

They are concentrations of your passions, sourced by your experiences

Where dependence has no cost, yet every body's paid

Family has supplied most of you, with the omission of your soul

Your very particular gift from God, stamps you as His child

The clay family line was the soil of your nurturing

We need our soil to hold us while we grow

There are complicating elements, but focus should stay in view

We will be judged for our work, not our bloodline

Here is where family began, we may speak with God, as His child

There is no legacy which farther gifts a soul forever

Family value, our bread crumbs to home

Focus of the Living

By C D Johnson

Long before this time, all the worlds' souls have once declared their will

But this gifted opportunity holds open our entry to His house

The sanction of spiritually hearing, was not meant for every clay

To digest with understanding, labels the blessings of the hearing

As followers, we are silently marked by advantage

This house is built on faith, for those who believe

When our lives run askew of our plans, hear the lessons of your growth

Failure to respond to that which you already know, can be our undoing

According to teaching from the Holy Bible

The wife of Lot, refused warning of their hazard

Choosing to turn back to what she knew, to her demise

This person may have acted out of alarm

But no matter her panic, she characterized one who would not hear

We are all needlessly too near a destiny of the salt pillar

Don't search for coded meanings when our treasure is to obey

Our expended life focus, dictates the delimiter of our work

The obscure defiance of the salted need not lead to your doom

Hero

By C D Johnson

The safeguarding of your affections, inherits a vast capacity to grow

While seeking protection from life alone, every option is your prize

When good spirits touch your connection, we walk stronger by our number

If solitary status drags heavily around your life, resolve is at your hand

Blessings adhere to our lives, as we're closer to our work

For the committed, so sources our strength

Trials abandon their threat to your joys, when smiles begin from inside

Frame of mind during our testing, graduates our journey

Stay firm in your endurance, to facilitate eternal growth

Not all boundaries are your limits, reach the pinnacle that you are

For a loved one in need your strength, the time to provide is as you know

Be thankful for fortunes unearned, they're perks of your belief

Recognize you've been loved, with depth enough to share

And sharing is what a hero does, grow strong in your comfort of another

When we emulate our learning, we express love of the Master

Father has shown us how

I Call You Esau

By C D Johnson

** Bonus entry **

We descend from wonderful people forged stronger than ourselves

With time, our treasured standards are reclaimed home

Our forbearers shouldered burdens set aside for punished beasts

Focused by fear, they tilled forward for to struggle is to live

Besieged every hour, heroic accomplishments define each day

But the things they knew as vital gave them faith

Prolonged hours further disrespected their insufficient rewards

Less than justice for their family fair

But our portions served were hungrily received

Reminded daily that these insufficient rewards, could be earned by someone else

Existing simply for survival, in time pennies grew to bills

Small dollars combined for a down payment on a home with your name

A place to mark your safety and be your address to the world

Now you are the heir of the transfer of your family growth

When are the blessings with your name not yours?

Time for the magnanimous sharing in you is not the time you feel

With the pressures of little funding, this too is a color of fear

You hold up though your family loss, but is this the aid you need?

The old family house must be exchanged for comfort

What else should you do when your time of need is now?

Should you bleed decades of new blood wealth spent for these few bricks?

Is the price you are too willing to spend meant for the children?

I call you Esau

You find life an option with your legacy as trade

Pain extended to gain a family base exchanged for an effortless meal

You show no perception that the edge you weld cuts deeply in both ways

Your family hemorrhages most for the accommodation consumed by the greedy

Is there a sign naming your ease to be grander than your child's

The same restraint of those who earned the first dollar

Remains open to those who are blessed in turn

If I could

By C D Johnson

To trust that we know the answer is calming to our uncertainty

Par for this course, this is how insecurity functions

When we think we know, it makes us less afraid

It would be so incredible if we would learn by the spoken word

A child fingering a hot stove, responses certainly from the heat not the warnings

This painful truth condemns us to reliving the missteps of our parents

Burns on our forefathers should protect by way of our learning

The need to personally be burned defies that we are smart

We hear love ones' words of counsel, but we need feel for ourselves

If I could

I would give the act of learning the equivalent of sex

Where lessons learned caused you endorphin inspired addictive rewards

The kind that makes you feel that you're where you alt to be

If addiction is the necessary tool, your work is too hard

During your life you may be blessed with guidance

Not all sources are equal, but listening just takes time

The choice is yours, but there may be a shield by deliberation

Before steps backward must become your advancement

The added consideration may leave you a more learned soul

Minimizing the yet to be known is as a blind man walking a cliff

Not all small mistakes are inclined remain small

I would help your understanding of this, if I could

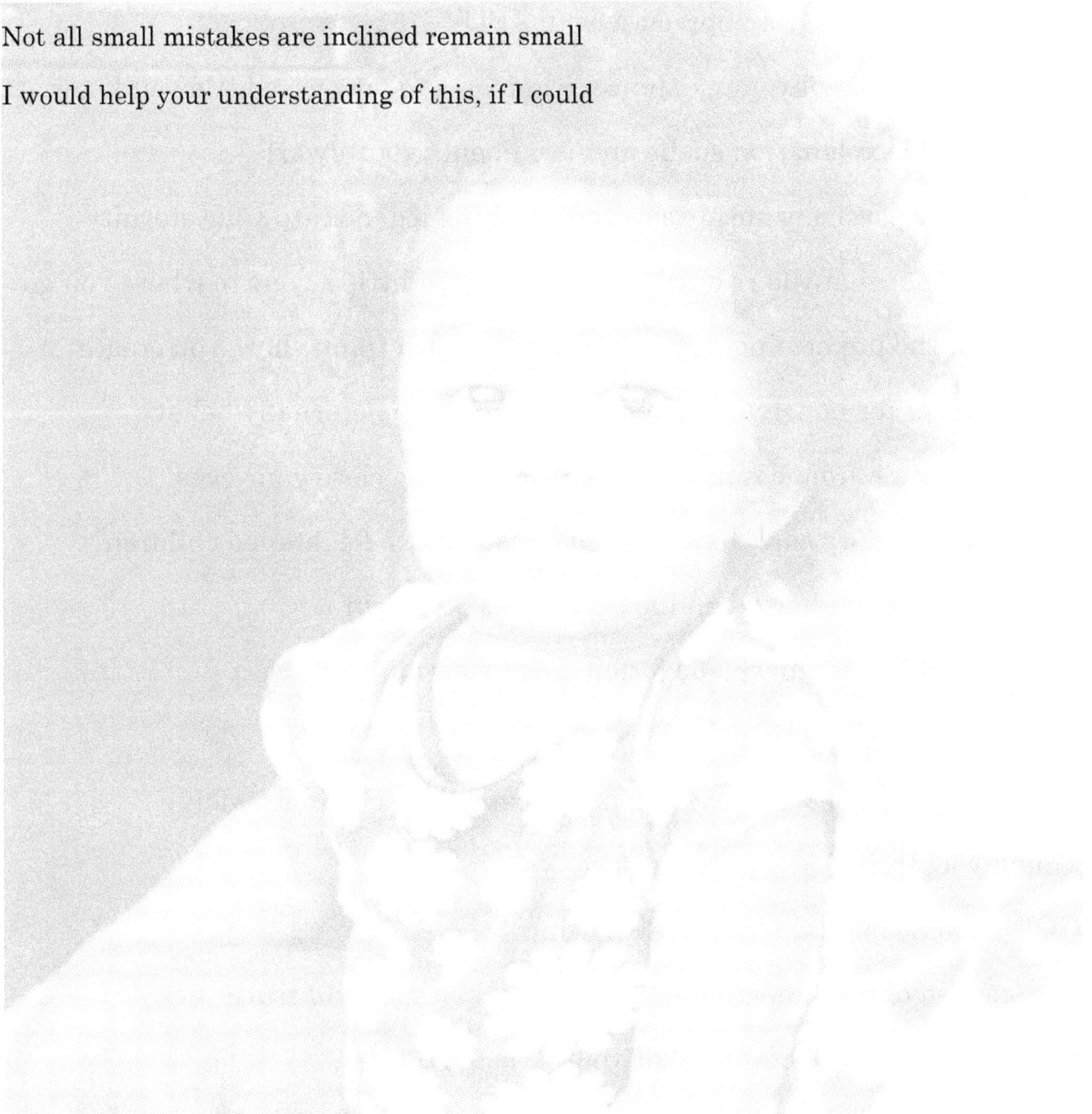

If this is your heaven

By C D Johnson

If this is your heaven, I appreciate your grief

When the summit of your existence, translates to how very little you know

Your evasive explanation spells and documents your dwarf

Within your psyche, your miracle lives etching legend into your eternity

It matters not that you're only a passenger with little say as to where you go

Mankind, the unknowing, dictates you take truth from where you create

 Punishment for impertinent, endangers those who eternally believe

Your protection from damnation may be to simply close your eyes

What you don't see can't hurt you, gives courage to frightened children

We can be so child like when life calls on us be grown

Closing your view can well be forfeiture of your option

GOD made way for every child

Without regard for where we began, we can all reach home safely

Thank you JESUS

GOD's love is not limited to the knowing

I've learned of fulfillments that complete every spiritual truth

You can know of life beyond that you've tasted

But you first must include your work among the Lord's one third

Fear is limited to the level of the breathing

GOD's reality makes us aware of real, without fear

Inmate mentality

By C D Johnson

From desperately drawing original breaths, just to allow you to scream

We arrived fighting, with the determination of the insane

Tiny struggles to clamp on an experience, they do not yet know

We choose the sensations of our continuance, without learned reason why

We're reaction driven by stimuli, beyond this understanding

This scenario is destined to dominate life for years, if you are blessed

An uncomfortable alternative can set far worst as your fate

Where life segments are measured by every blessed breath

Waiting the fall of the other shoe, suffers as final as a verdict of guilt

The product of the caged, is edged with the repercussions of lives

Each cage bears its own stench, cages construct as personally as our mirror

You may not be restrained from your travels

But your soul can still endure your chains

We source excitement for our labor, fulfilling fresh our need for keys

There will be trials or there will be lessons

You may select your point of view

The painful moments we would wish away, have the same value of the best

Timing can list us as victims, but direction forms our defense

If forces restrict your body, allow faith to advance your spirit

The feeling of our helplessness, does not make it so

God is the power that frees us from our bonds, when our hearts believe

This ordeal should be the ace we need, we're given the single answer

Essences' adjusts with the direction of our focus

No one can cage your totality,

   without the contribution of your hand

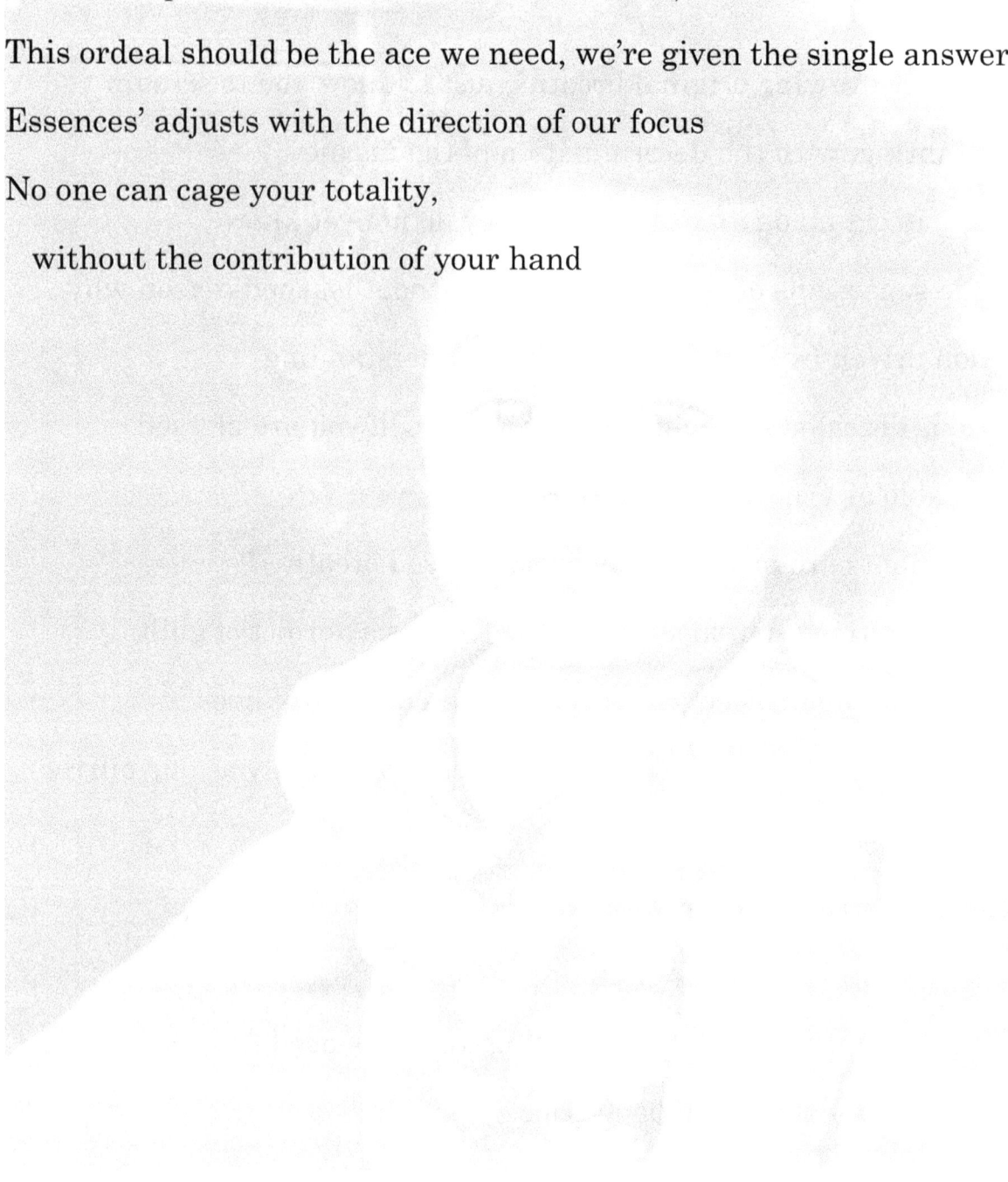

Just because

By C D Johnson

The recollections of my seedling growth,

 marked me content with the world I'd met

Introductions had been few,

 but we are thankful for the very soil, which facilitates fruition

We were expected to be content with consistency, never to see advantage

My people chose Gods' teachings, clay death fits longevity best

Black people have walked with Jesus, faith documented with our blood

Decisions we nurtured as a people, fixed our focus beyond those years

The villages remembered still, the family way we teach

The leadership of the man, equaled by the lady who grew our minds

Families were our system, to teach that we believe

But although given the answer, our questions still continue

We must be fateful to our beliefs, when we do believe

Some biblical lessons warn our lives of whores

We choose to miss understand, that the question is to whom you pray

Just because you feel safe via the torture of your siblings

This clay existence is populated by clay people, safety is your myth

But just because this life is trying, it provides thrust for you to try

Because God maintains His children in His view, just because

Like Minds

By C D Johnson

When seeking a love partnership, the sense with priority is sight

Few people find pride in this antiquated weakness,

 Still its' an attribute of our whole

The greatest danger and the most likely complication is, denial

As an effort to self elevate, we fail to examine the source of our error

There are many concerns in our day to day, we often times simply act

This is the definition for the blind and confused

Yet this is not reason for shame, more an acknowledge of self

The critical first step for we the confused, is recognition

There will always be moves that can be made, but to what end?

For two lives to navigate their run in parallel,

Their destinations will not be guaranteed

Each mind is likely to envision its own path

With no attempt at falsehood, like hearts are not always like minds

Talk with them, with all the urgency of your happiness

If there is a shared spirit, you have opportunity

Love Sense

By C D Johnson

To realize possibilities, requites you release bogus control

It feels empowering to spiel aloud about the staying of our resolve

We proudly declare to our elders about how we've come of age

Simultaneous declarations to the children that they are too fresh to know

The more similar the psyche, the wider the breach

Sometimes everyone is right, and then again no one is

Right can be relative to where it is you start

If the words that you've been faced with, digs scars into your heart

This is when love must dwarf your pain

To answer back with wounding, not your path to go

You need to hold love ones to your heart, agreement has a way

There is great danger when we begin to close our doors

Closed doors mark a barrier we may not defeat

Difficult discussions are impossible to ignore

There is no lesson when the class is destroyed for example

You are composed of the collected circles of your love ones

You can no more end your caring than you understand why you feel as you do!

Do not try to demonstrate how little it is you care, only how very much

The hands that you push away may be needed to fetch your last water and close your eyes

By way of love

Make a joyful noise

By C D Johnson

Before you reside in happiness, appreciate the blessing

While joy is undefined to your heart, it is unknown to your possibility

We squirm with all that we are, not every effort advances

As an infant screams with all its fury, when what he needs is sleep

Our young responses grow our difficulty, in the like of the child

To believe people crave a bumped head, examine your life

Your fear is where your future goes to fade

GOD paints your blessings lucid

Some concerns are as grave as our clay death

, but importance is not your anxiety

That which our souls need, is never determined by dread

When the path is laid by GOD, your way is certain

Give great voice, with all that you are for your blessings

Trumpet your thankfulness for gifts so personal and unique

If you await the signal to praise HIM

, the sounds of your joy may be what you've been waiting to hear

March of the lemming

By C D Johnson

The rules for our engagement, are most locally defined

Where the actions that we perceive, are the limits to that we see

And pigeon-holing every spirit, forms a proxy for our understanding

We follow in line with clay madness

, garnering all the loyalty of your surrender

 Keeping the insanity you've known secure, makes a fool feel safe

While your safety is seriously streaming farther away

Mostly without the consideration, that we would give something serious

The fact that someone stands before you, does not name your guide

The trail of those who walk just ahead, offer few clues for your direction

Every life decision should pass the test of your faith

Even with trial, take no path that's not toward the Son

When your thoughts begin with the search for ease

, discomfort is scheduled for your learning

The results of our actions can dig holes in our garden

Too many holes will leave less room to grow

We will have need to fed from this garden

Take care with your choice of lead

Mulligan

By C D Johnson

For we the idle masochist with addiction to the game of golf

Our mind melding chance to just hit something is enabling

The comfort level, sometimes, renders the scoring, selective

When an errant effort fails to do us service, we call for a mulligan

No matter our faults, mistakes can be retried

And with the speed of amnesia, the ill struck endeavor never happened

Those without understanding, sometimes employ such protections

With the self infected failure of surrender

Genuine moments are tasted but once, with our results made final

Thankfully there is cake for the blessed each way

Your children are your mulligan, virgin perspectives offer fresh gifts

For your person, become the person that you will admire every day

There is a heart filled satisfaction sleeping deep within your reach

When we learn to scrutinize home, more so than the neighbor

, our efforts are grown in the real light

There is no elevation for us in throwing others at our feet

The actual facts of our lives, never adjust for our comfort

So adjust your level of comfort to the test

My choice

By C D Johnson

The furthermost of these lessons, requites fresh knowledge of our need

Necessity targets the energies, but fails comprehension of our journey

The options of selective truths stay limited by objective

If you drink of the blood for your purity, purity spikes your flavor

Life direction is the private vehicle of your steering

Satanic conclusions will only dell where the boutique is theirs

Remain the first line of your own defense

When you can be of good service, your actions should be destiny

There will always be compensation, no matter the direction of your act

When ill-conceived thoughts take hold as reality, you're lead by suggestion

Give great thought to where you stand, all responses mark your concussion

We can't look for evenness of exchange, this life's' about gifts you can't repay

Payment scheduled for your need, gives life to your duration

Stealing joy from distressed siblings, labels membership of the third

This life stage is your declaration

Make thoughtfully clear your choice, because it's yours

My neighbors' yard

By C D Johnson

Escape sometimes, makes feasible another day

Time is the defining element of our duration

But when we disguise the truth about our values

We hide within fantasies of our worth

Lies of imagination, we wear like a clinging stench

Attributes we pretend not to notice

Where is your respect for your neighbor's house?

While you study the body of his wife

  , there is no righteousness in calling him brother

When you should be lifted by your own appreciation, you envy

The beauty of the woman never justifies when we covet

Constraint of your lust should by your respect

We are all gifted personally, beginning with our own seed

The blessings of one life forge unlike meanings for his brother

The perfect fit for our parts is determined by our God

Your treasures in life live within your house

You don't need to fence the yard to discover what is yours

Name your price

By C D Johnson

Bartering for necessities, affords thoughts of our contribution

Survival of these clay vessels, mothers our courage and cowardice by reflex

When given choice between loss of great value and the unfortunates of pain

Our response is more individual than DNA and defended with greater furor

We have selected recall of our extremes, hedging guards against our fear

There can always be such loss, that defeats your bravery without a shot fired

I cannot equally comprehend the grief of my brother, but I hurt as well

When the desperation of a homeless mother is hidden, we can quietly see

As victims of our radiation of compassion, we share

Recalling the biblical story of Abraham and his fear of great loss

Presented with the obedience to GOD or the death of his son

His choice must be made clear, with the heavy heart of the child-less

His faith kept him strong in his belief

Our feelings, for the feelings of our existence, keep our heart in peril

The price for our salvation was the clay death of my Lord and Savior

The price feels too high, without equal return

Our tidal response requires all of you

If you know your debt, you may also know your way

Now I lay me down to sleep

By C D Johnson

Have the actions for my comfort, been of labor of my faith

I pray for correction, ever as my corrects prove ongoing

GOD's children have blessings beyond our work

Fortunate for lives of limited reach

But we know with all our certainty, that there is more

Now I lay me down to sleep

I pray the LORD, my soul to keep

If I should die before I wake

Some words spoken as children, we are to never out grow

You were made safe by your belief in small prayers

Sight illuminates your protection in force, but belief makes it real

This is not our home, but here we've got work to do

Our efforts are where joy is defined as our own

And as for time, our time will be as we've been told

Live well; the days of the shell are in your pasted time

Young birds are often reluctant to fly but flying makes them birds

The conclusion of this existence begins forever, believe in your prayers

No matter the time, completion is solely by the LORD's grace

One Expectation of Seeds

By C D Johnson

This cycle of our continuance, illuminates the divinity of His love

As we humanly learn to teach, the enormity of our ignorance, frustrates

The frustration of the immature, marks the first softening of their will

In the way the patience of parents, marks the level they have grown

To disallow our challenge, revives the foolishness of our comfort

We expect, the light of our teaching to produce a finer fruit than ourselves

There is little notice that the purity of the message has changed

The realization that we are better equipped to listen, than to speak

, gives us foundation for when we have need to be more

Our own strength is our focus

Even when we error, we have our path for correction

The love of our correction, is the entirety of what a parent expects

Personal Perception

By C D Johnson

We blindly gather personalized truths of the day

Distinguishing between the flavors of consideration and distain

Transforming our heap into a hardening filter of our exposures

Just as an unknowing child learns of life's bruising by experience

We tend to believe most, the things that we have been touched by

This first level of protection services well for our minority

 , but as we've learned, we should know

There are some choices of direction that will not serve you well

Sometimes we see things coming, often knee deep unaware

No matter the depth of your trial, your court has a friend

Allow the shield of your belief, to extend your understanding

You need not ignore your fearful reactions

But make your faith your filter

With the guidance of GOD, your perception is on point

Rivals

By C. D. Johnson Sr.

Most scenarios of pleasing comfort, exist for your enslavement

The jurisdiction for your options, are limited by your failing focus

This baseline acuity of the frighten is not pleasing

But some of the times, the paranoid are right

The conflict between good vs. evil is an actuality of time

Opposing purposes subsist, fiercely fed from contesting sources

Your complicating concern is that they both live within your will

It is crucial, that you distinguish the payer of your tuition

With whom do we converse when we talk things out with ourselves?

The familiar voice you receive into your thoughts

  , an ideal you may have had in passing

The possibilities of the world are illustrated, as the limitless will of GOD

Children fed limited views, function with partial learning

When a lie is used to build esteem, the attempt is short sighted

A child has modest dexterity with one size fits all

We sometimes perceive anxiety in the ways of the child

Our focus loses clarity when ill conceived responses do conflict

Our blessed recognition is made more difficult when the battle is us

You must always be a resource of your correction

There is no other housekeeping more crucial for your best

Questioning yourself, is not solely a flaw of the undecided

As in a maze, every direction taken resolves your future options

It is life defining as to which rival you adhere to

Source of Conviction

By C D Johnson

Everything of worth that comes to you, comes to you at some cost

Obtuse realism feels deflowering but the truth is your light

Even positive attachments expect to extract their fee

Some connections evolve from relaxed to symbiotic

Mother don't ask a fee, when they house their coming child

When the cost is too great to be spoken

It must just be thankfully accepted

Experienced couples, clutch closely against the challenging winds

It makes them feel strong, even when strong is not what they are

Not every circumstance conforms to our dreams

In exchange, action moves both ways

Elders would say that "a fair exchange ain't no robbery"

Understanding that when we receive, it sets the stage for our donation

You'll find no detriment in knowing to whom it is you owe

Truth justifies the vast depth of such attachments

Although our beginning is one of my need

My heart tells me that this like GOD's gentle hand, incubating my soul

Existence with no understanding can make the vulnerable a fool

With all that GOD has provided, what is your exchange?

If you love being loved, the limits are set by you

No matter your devotion, the exchange cannot be the same

The love of GOD is without boundary, we must thankfully accept

When there is no equal, find joy in your role

The FATHER gives us everything we have, to be everything we can

Sparkles are for children

By C D Johnson

Expectations commence with our eyes, we crave particular visions as special

The forte forces a typical response from similar atypical victims

The fixation on possibilities unknown, tends to manufacture new fools

Although the manufacturing of our foulness has been our byproduct

The lady of attraction can be any lady, thru particular eyes

The twinkle that causes your ignition, was intended for your view

Proving susceptible to the vermin, tags you one of many

The clay is responding to a function of these forms, that's how we're made

Directed by hormones, we literally speed without sight

The learning of our years gets the cold disrespect of a senile uncle

We require a stronger purpose to retain our focus

But we must first have one

Just floating between your days, lends your participation in problems

Some actions should carry more meaning than some others

So thinking ahead to your next frame

Sparkles don't show the same in real light

To delight in entertainment, neither makes you sinner or fool

Adults comfort in light to keep our lane

We can be entertained by blinking lights just as children

But an adult drive to feel like as a child, can disrupt our thinking

The fantasies of imagination, confuses the genius with the mad

While our reality lives mortified, somewhere between

The vital lesson for this experience is to find your way home

Shiny things will sometimes cause us to error

But the knots on head are fashioned by you

If you feed from beliefs that leave you in starvation, you need adjust

The shadows of your questions come to light, when we ask

The communication you search for is one on one, and GOD waits your call

Don't be distracted by sleight of hand, there's' a man behind the curtain

Gods' warmth is assurance, where there is only demise

We can all be misled, but here is where adjustment comes in

If you strayed from your path, have that talk and come home

Parents forgive, and our Father is the One parent of all

Where the glitter is gold and the light is eternal

Spoiled fruit

By C D Johnson

Laundering the contents of our spirit, often wears for us as stifling

There's a strong requisite to circumvent your chosen path

You pray for Christian thoughts but growth dwells within your options

There will need to be more light before we see

Take notice of the manner of babies

They rock the tooth-less air of seniors and often times their wisdom

Their guard has not been fortified by paranoia and fear is yet unknown

They embody love in this earth worlds' most pure vessel

Why must they change, is it protection we feel that they must covet?

The memory of our own disappointments celebrate our failures

This is a microcosm of our rotted perception of purgatory

The youth convey with courage, when they are allow to speak

Children expect wellbeing to be as the air, all will share

Our matured fears equip us to envision hell before we can see heaven

Is seems that hell is easier to conceive

But why when we began so well?

Termination Infection

By C.D. Johnson

When the access that we've reveled in, is unalterably tainted

This marrow deep detachment only affords us the humanity of loss

Anguish precipitated overhead with coverage of a fathoms depth

This time imposes a painful amendment to plans and design

Subsequent time seems to demand that meaningful effects be dissimilar

When we truly share, sharing is very special

But the list of special connections has been eternally abridged by one

Now consent to your emotional reprieve, because it's necessary

New is the necessity of progression, even with its' obligatory sting

The deep love you've felt is never lost, more saved

This aberration keeps us whole when we are deprived of a valued part

When there are favored kinships, there will be agonizing loss

These testes can be disabling but disability is not the need you have

This is time should be in thanks

Thanks that you have knowledge of such a compelling experience

For continuance, smile in your discomfort although there is little comfort in this goodbye

Quietly deafening sentiments fester, filling your head with thoughts you dare not feel now

It's complicated to share that which we've not yet internalized as real

Demonstrating resolve is expected, awkward and asking too much

We customize our grief with the instruction of our experience, as best we can

But this is no minor annoyance, this infection demands some change

There is no preservation of self in caring

Love is the light you gleam for another

Simplify because you delight in their shine

There is an invidious connection that forms your universe as magic

The reasons for change remain, profound as the motives for your clay experience

Not every torment is overtly targeting your heart

Sometimes, change is just a very difficult graduation

Love within your circle is embossed on every instant shared

Just as GOD declared His love for His children is ever lasting, as is love

That's my dog

By C D Johnson

My Fathers' children develop common feelings for shared questions

Family ties get rooted beyond bloodlines, but explained by what we believe

Loyalty, equates with the clay, with the godliness of trust

Your choice of pet to greet you home, says a ton about your comfort

Some pet family is always excited, just to see you home

We enjoy the company of different friends, even those with tails

Friendships fortify our number, but mostly grow assurance

Even the threat to succeeding breaths, keep some connections strong

We face challenges to our continuance, but mostly thru our folly

The consistency that you crave, shapes a better question of your actions

The clay demand trust and loyalty, from those that they do service

Yet we dig with swallow consideration, for the love that we return

If you require more, than you've got to give, you dwell as a cat

Recognition can be painful, that how birthing feels

We are not dogs or cats, so expectations must be better

When you ignore suffering, of one within your reach

Feelings and your actions for sibling defines what you are

The Allure of Woman

** Bonus entry **

The gift of a woman's nearness seeds your surrender

Without her touch we mourn the grief of a thousand tears

She embodies the refuge we knew, the haven we seek

When the darkness grew our fear, her loving hands calm the young heart

When the young world seemed to crumble, a maternal embrace had great power

We relate these feelings, security with love and it make us feel safe

No other inducement has such power of completion and of void

To even drag weaker souls, willfully from the heavens

The essence of woman can never be unseen

The love of mother and that for any other is different by objective

But a persons' dependence can evolve in the same way

Old Testament lessons teach warnings about strange women

But the influence of the body exchange, lives deeper than touch

We are attracted to shiny things

Things different from us

Treasuring the shiny will afford testes that you may not pass

We are so blinded by the twinkle; we fail to notice that it's not really a star

Let's not further spread the propaganda, that strange means woman alone

No, making clay mistakes is likely for us all

Living in one treasured night is not having the spark to burn or good reason to ignite

Strange is loving someone who has a different heart than yours

The trails before you, you can never travel in tandem

Messages become obstacles when they aren't received aligned

If the partner in your life bows to other than you do, this is more than strange

You must believe with your soul where it is you need to go

The allure for strange clay, is itself strange

Think of it this way

By C. D. Johnson

To embody the ways of the shepherd

Defines the impossible dream

We crave inclusion for battle we do not yet understand

And still praying for protections, against the trials of our bruising

Your response is an automated declaration of how you feel

Some have no option but to protect

Core believes are structure, since before we fed from the breast

We steer, especially if we're uncertain we know the way

The unyielding, mandates corrections for the fortunate

Even those who don't know they've been so blessed

The fork in the road comes with both options and consequences

If the children are deprived of its community milk

Support and understanding become merely a child's yearning

When the community shows strength by the back of its hand

We discard the treasure along with the sand

Our existence is more blessed to salvage the child than to cage the man

Think of it this way

Some people believe that they live the love of GOD

They think of love, in the terms of the dust

Fear the price of our unknowing, without the fear of our failure

The relative possibilities for each soul, should be initiated by faith

Wisdom dictates we accommodate and appreciate our blessings

The defining empowerment of your will, is your belief

There's no enduring power in our infantile hands of clay

 , but there is all faculty with the love of GOD

While perfection is not within us, it must continue to be our goal

Just as you position your child's first step, equal to winning a race

Remember, GOD is your connection with perfection

And he sees greatness, in the tiny gains we make

If you failure to connect, understand the way of your problem

Treasured Demons

By C. D. Johnson

Because of the gravitational attraction to her charms

, there is obstruction to what you see

The distraction from her form, displaces sight with adolescent hormones

Her compliments roll in, deeply kissing the ring

Self-enslavement to her icon, has well become her capturer

Seeking her warmth, where her fire is being fed, memories from guttural old minds

Her essence disrupts your self control but that was always her intent

The fact of her existence mothers tension for the depraved

, but some creations of awe are simply people

Vanity is a most fervent, consuming demon

More powerful than as a persons' love of self

But if you lay victim to the vanity of someone else

, compensation thru attachment has you mislead

It takes both hands to safely steer your course

, we have no sway over the life of someone else

No matter the demons at your gate, stay your lane

Appreciation does not make an ideal

Treasured

By C D Johnson

My most darling child

You shape my love dilemma, and I'm thankful

Temptation grows in me still, to tend to you as my focus

But the focus of this house has many rooms to service, none more than you

I take great pride in the maturation of your spirit

You're forcing my growth to try and keep your pace

You are not my sole child, but I love you with a singular feeling

I requite your good welfare before I can breathe

I breathe deeply our family essences, blood flows thicker than the stone

With our comparative comprehension of love askew

Imagine if the number of your children were as the grains of sand

Would your heart be large enough for what our Father must feel?

A totally unfair request, to be compared with God, but we must try

No matter from where we start, from whom we start is our strength

We must embrace the impossible challenge, morphing in to more than we are

Of this world, no love is greater than between parent with child

As you consider this, give thanks to your Father

Unassuming Instrument

By C D Johnson

The humble heart can never be the house for malicious

As the institution of Satan, holds no power within these vessels

When your concerns are those of right, you identify your core

If this concept has no meaning for you, this identifies as well

The order of service begins with whom you serve

Believers learn to applaud the flight of family, as the breath of life

Only the Reverent is above the understanding and confusion of the clay

Fear not your performance to date, but there will be an end of this time

When your response is presented with the sharing of a clinched fist

You've closed your future to the possibilities of this tomorrow

This does not smear you as lost, the task remains within your hand

There is little as securing as the righteousness of our own feelings

The thoughts consumed unspoken, as well as when we talk as a fool

There will certainly be mistakes, but errors mark the path of the child

Correction depends on the content of your own belief

The meek and humble **will** inherit because all will learn to be humble

We clay of no power, continue blessed by inheritance, be thankful

Virtually Virgin

By C. D. Johnson

Purity has nothing to do with white or snow

To desire some value for ourselves, is a part of this role we live

Few of us can distinguish between, the different carats of gold

, but the number '24' starts an ingrown smile

For this earth world, a gifts importance is relative its giver

When a gift of love makes its way to a dutiful parent

, the contents have no equal

Your life is a lot like that gift

The grass that you see as greener, for you, is not as sweet

Do not try to compare with other gifts, that which is meant for you is yours

Our sole gift of purity, is more than two centuries old

We have no like present for us to return

, but a lesser offering is the least GOD should receive

Perfection is neither our trial nor a suitable journey for these vessels

The purity of our spirit, requires our ongoing clearing of dust

There will be imperfect times, but bad times don't last

Each moment we live, we are gifted with the opportunity to be clean

An opportunity to be virgin children again

Walking the ledge

By C D Johnson

Balance prolongs this experience, and renders texture to this serving

We are tasked with our growth, from our sun deprived and water less feeding

Preparing for our future tests the merit of the moment

, as if we walk a ledge, one step must be firmly planted before the next

The path of the ledge, is seldom linear for our ease

The serial motion is confusion, with obstacles of your psyche homemade

Our efforts to prove that we can handle it all, but all, can prove too much

We abruptly awake to our source of strength, as we overtly sport the gray

The pace of your lessons is dictated by the depth of your faith

But even believes paths can be encumbered

When children fear the monsters of their closet, they call out for their father

It is never that mothers' love won't do, but what fathers live for

The problems forming monsters in your closet have an answer that you know

Call on your Father

Walking the ledge to your completion will require His help

God has lived and died for your privilege

Welcomed pursuit

By C D Johnson

Serious addiction sacrifices breathing, for the hope of the next breath

Dependent experiences attach personally, as specifically as essence

Spawning in innumerable flavored convulsions, the functions work the same

No matter your choice of dependency, you're being sold

Derived is there must be an elite energy, to power ones so weak to be strong

This world has developed disabling skills to deny our strength

Right now, making it to the sun, sounds nearly like success

But to those who dwell in the dimness, a smile can be a beacon

Every addiction garners its own reaction

From acknowledging pats on the back to your faith deep damnation

Most reputations are earned, but each stand by its own power

Notions of your treasure are diluted by a fresh toy

If drugs are your passionate lover, you're getting no love from your passion

You feel personally crushed that the emperor has no cloths

The fault must be that of someone who controls your right and wrong

When it is you who have no eyes to see, and little knowledge of your blindness

The product of your work, smolders deep within your future

True devotion is an irrevocable directive that originates at your soul

By way of the choices you make, you decree your pursuit

What do you do?

By C D Johnson

(Note to the married man)

When the stimulation that you crave stupid, Is the next worst choice in your life

Pending betrayal will not be blamed on your drink

Some flights of fantasy, are only meant to be that

Think about the things you can't undo

Unattached strings entangle the unaware, unaware as in fool

If growing up remains high on your list, time to put that to your test

This moment is a unicorn

A decision that extends beyond the pain that we perceive

All of the intricacies have their own funky favor

But the implosion you are implanting, has been poison to love before

Remember unicorns need not be real

Harming those who are vested, pursuing sensation you do not know

The volume of considerations that scare you,

 speak volumes for the content of your heart

There is no gain in cultivating a field which is not yours

Lust applauds the danger of this fools moment

With a connection measured by the length of a fools tools

An unimportant trophy, denoting achievements in selfishness

You need protect from the moments after

When the light comes on and the 'roaches' scramble

You can be the rock for your house, or the first stone casted

When you decide that which makes you a man, then you know

A man must be thorough for his work to be complete

Your room is a function of the greater house

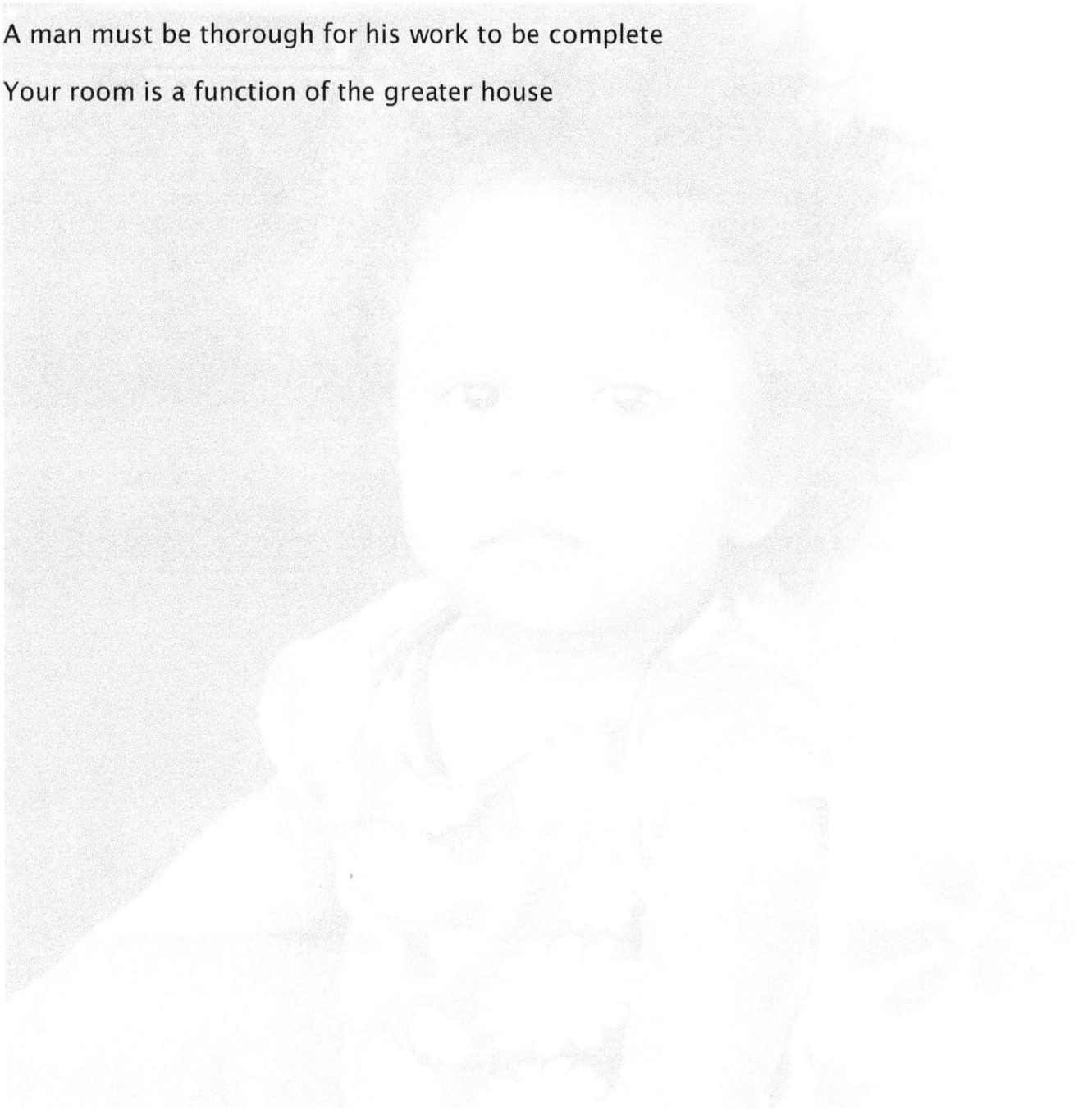

What feels good to you...

By C D Johnson

We were created in the image of perfection

Perfection can never be less, it is the definition of splendor

But being graced with His image does not advance our meager merit

Without the love, our existences are fools' dreams of grandeur

We've been generously gifted with options we try not to understanding

The quiet expectation to advance our worth, is truly only stout for some

You own the option to be unsuccessful in your understanding

Souls who grasp the question, rudders their own vessel

This earth world introduces addicting sensations to these clay bodies

Sensations so addictive, that our submission is our contribution

Everything about us is the way we're meant to be, both our strength and our faults

We mallet out the persons, we envision as correct

The complication to our harmony is from those of a different happiness

Some who have dissimilar goals because they give service to a dissimilar alter

The persons with whom you share your life, should also share your work

Each soul will account for their personal declaration of need

If you need a selected touch more than your elevation, then pray to discern your need

We may hormonally choose to our error, but recognize a choice is being made

When the man loves like a mother

** Bonus entry **

The nearest we're gifted with love bleeds maternal

These angels live for these commitments without fear

Endurance without regret, no requisite or pity tears

The vaginal link can manifest a perpetually open hand

 , but not every hand

There are those who cannot see their lives because of how they live

There are producers who solely celebrates the production over the product

They may have purpose for the moment but moments are quickly memories to come

The dependent face of child translates to stress from the past not joy for their future

Blessedly, not all angels are female

There are young fathers who become men purely by their fresh station

Within strong men there is a brutish bridled force, their love

Feelings kept in check for fear of being misunderstood or understood too well

But the focus of fathers should be understood as well

When you see a good dad taking his child to school; the hugs crush a little tight and last a little long

Vigorously preaching, repeating cautions for the day, but this is how they protect

Reacting too much to any pending ill but this is how they love

Paternal love can be a beast unto its self but even beasts respect devotion

The true fathers would give their lives to protect but this often censors their smile

There are few forces as willing and none who would give more, anything to safeguard their line

So, how can you question the love of our Heaven Father?

Because all about GOD is good

When you wear that mask

The scenario that animates us best, features life on fire

Performing the life tasks forced at issue

Or servicing our caste prerequisite of earned paranoia

We require a higher motivation to set scrutiny on self

Effortlessly cultivating tailored protections for our soft places

It is as if we expected perfection from this imperfect source

Seek the truth; ignoring fear manifests its hold

The profound reek proves its self corrosive to the future

When you feel the need to lash out with your fury

Or warning to the world that you're near to loss control

Make time to match the offense with your demonstration

You are responding to your uncertainty with surrender

Not every challenge has your name

Your test may be misunderstood

The actually brave demonstrate that the fury is a disservice

Adoring the 'mask of your edge' balances your work on a meager surface

We should not bequeath our potency because another wants to see

Or make our hype the mind-set of our actions

Release yourself from frighten panic

It documents your discomfort and reduces your face

The control that we absolutely must retain is of self

Never allow outside noise to obscure the music you are playing

Your sounds direction your focus, your focus defines your work

Confrontation is too often the required task before you

But the brave cannot persist behind the mask and remain brave

We must be creatures of our work

Especially if it is logical to have thoughts beyond this moment

When thoughtless actions become the architect the future

We design our devastation within of our plan

WHO FINGERS YOUR REMOTE?

By C D Johnson

Control is the orgasm of folk with options

While the rest father addictions where there is no supply

Our clay madness, favors reality switchable by emotion

Mating desire with need, but never matching

False wisdom manipulates our understanding, to make foolishness real

There are no comparative numbers before a dream becomes a thing

Loss of way gleams our misunderstanding

As we cultivate need to take the wheel, we who cannot drive

Your love touches entirely, more personally than mere words

The uncontrolled quiver triggers the measured fan of your gate

This moment is special, to the exclusion of its scrutiny

It is difficult to know if you should wind down or burn-up

To use your partner for yourself is not love

Masturbation by friendship, seeking a deep answer from a shallow response

Clay orchestrate necessities, which channel direction to parts unknown

Destinations made bitterly irrelevant by casual priorities

When the moment puts your path in amendment, recalculate

The worth of your aspirations should reset your consideration

But when the thumping of your pulse, is really your objective

You're experiencing your focus as if a movie

Whore

By CD Johnson

The Bible pre-recorded the pathway this experience will tread

The teachings exposed diverse concerns and warnings of our jeopardy

One such warning spoke to us employing the word whore

That term exposes a revelation of discord, no matter your participation

The rudderless may father opportunity without connection

Many inherited a profile when the colors are too common

Such is our level of consideration, children wearing big shoes

The mention of whores, biblically, has little to do with interment exchange

The interaction of the clay is much less your trial

Your trial of your actions inquires, to whom do you pray

Have you ever needed a special moment that must be now?

When the intensity justifies, promises are as easily lost as clothing

We are as we've been made, but we shouldn't be less

Our interactions are not always sinful, but too often can be thought-less

GOD is the beginning and the end

HE must be our first thought as He will be our last

The prerequisite for salvation is the One Love

When your lifestyle is the engine that drives your work

You're kneeling at the wrong alter

If the conversation of your town intends to disrobes your neighbor

Your quiet allegiance is woefully misplaced

When your worth emanates from the things that you can buy

Recognize that you can never buy your worth

The monogamy between The LORD and his children

Allows no comparable attachment

If you are directed by hungers, your faith cannot share

Pray for the contentment that makes you whole, the price has been paid

COPYRIGHT © 2018

ALL RIGHTS RESERVED. NO PART OF THIS BOOK MAY BE REPRODUCED OR TRANSMITTED IN ANY FORM OR BY ANY MEANS WITHOUT WRITTEN PERMISSION OF THE AUTHOR.

ISBN: 978-1-5323-8305-2

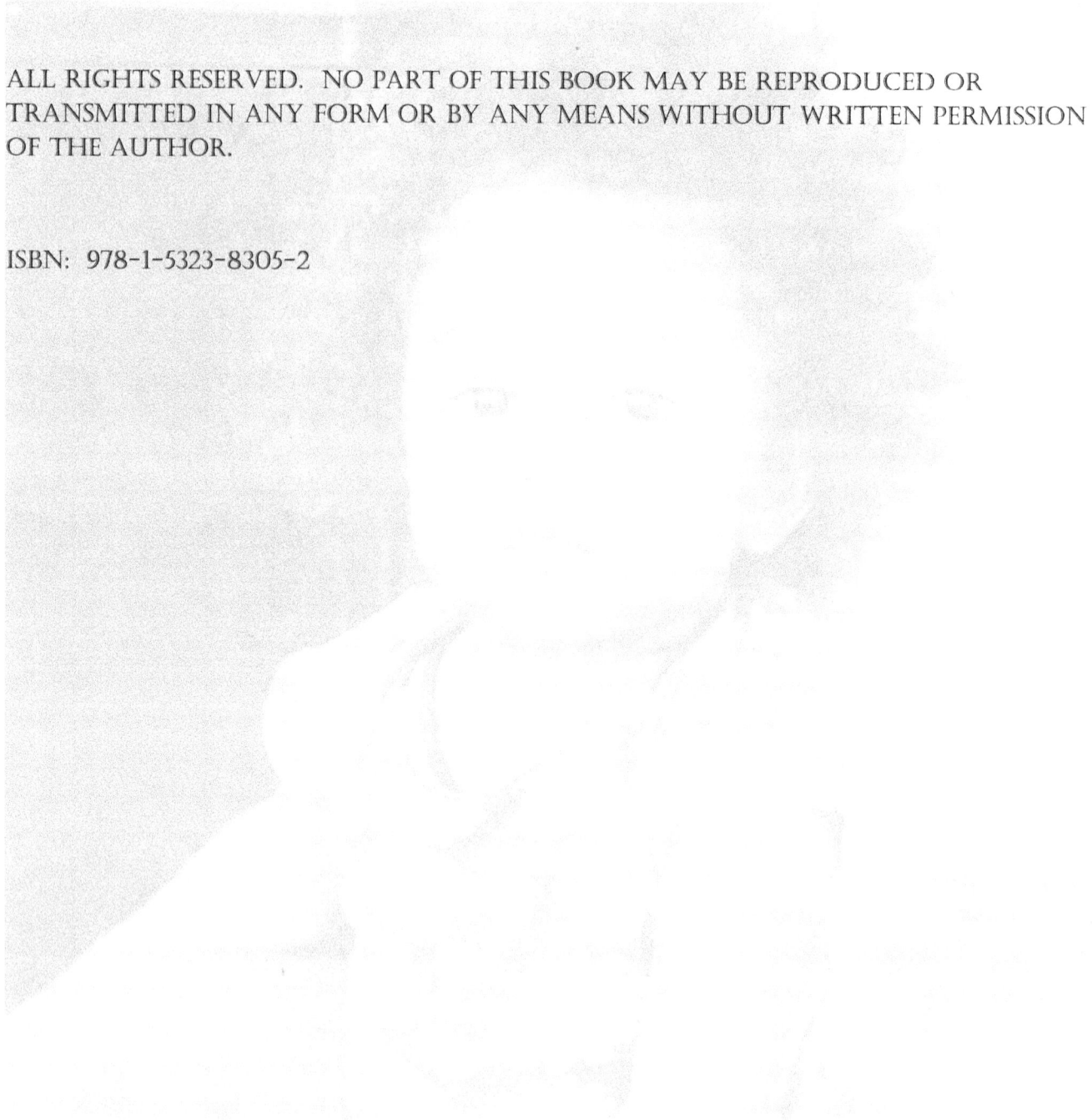

www.ingramcontent.com/pod-product-compliance
Lightning Source LLC
Chambersburg PA
CBHW050642150426

42813CB00054B/1153